FUNERAL FLOWERS

by Emma Dennis-Edwards

samuelfrench.co.uk

THINKING ABOUT PERFORMING A SHOW?

There are thousands of plays and musicals available to perform from Samuel French right now, and applying for a licence is easier and more affordable than you might think

From classic plays to brand new musicals, from monologues to epic dramas, there are shows for everyone.

Plays and musicals are protected by copyright law, so if you want to perform them, the first thing you'll need is a licence. This simple process helps support the playwright by ensuring they get paid for their work and means that you'll have the documents you need to stage the show in public.

Not all our shows are available to perform all the time, so it's important to check and apply for a licence before you start rehearsals or commit to doing the show.

LEARN MORE & FIND THOUSANDS OF SHOWS

Browse our full range of plays and musicals, and find out more about how to license a show

www.samuelfrench.co.uk/perform

Talk to the friendly experts in our Licensing team for advice on choosing a show and help with licensing

plays@samuelfrench.co.uk   020 7387 9373

Acting Editions
BORN TO PERFORM

Playscripts designed from the ground up to work the way you do in rehearsal, performance and study

---

Larger, clearer text for easier reading

Wider margins for notes

Performance features such as character and props lists, sound and lighting cues, and more

---

+ CHOOSE A SIZE AND STYLE TO SUIT YOU

 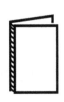 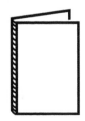

STANDARD EDITION	**SPIRAL-BOUND EDITION**	**LARGE EDITION**
Our regular paperback book at our regular size	The same size as the Standard Edition, but with a sturdy, easy-to-fold, easy-to-hold spiral-bound spine	A4 size and spiral bound, with larger text and a blank page for notes opposite every page of text – perfect for technical and directing use

MUSIC USE NOTE

Licensees are solely responsible for obtaining formal written permission from copyright owners to use copyrighted music in the performance of this play and are strongly cautioned to do so. If no such permission is obtained by the licensee, then the licensee must use only original music that the licensee owns and controls. Licensees are solely responsible and liable for all music clearances and shall indemnify the copyright owners of the play(s) and their licensing agent, Samuel French, against any costs, expenses, losses and liabilities arising from the use of music by licensees. Please contact the appropriate music licensing authority in your territory for the rights to any incidental music.

IMPORTANT BILLING AND CREDIT REQUIREMENTS

If you have obtained performance rights to this title, please refer to your licensing agreement for important billing and credit requirements.

ABOUT THE AUTHOR

Emma is a writer and performer of Jamaican and Trinidadian heritage, she trained as an actor at East 15 Acting School and has been part of a number of prestigious writing programmes with theatres such as the Royal Court, Soho Theatre and the Lyric Hammersmith. Her work has been performed at The Tricycle, Arcola, Royal Court and Ovalhouse.

Funeral Flowers was commissioned by Power Play Theatre Activists in association with the Pleasance Theatre and was part of the Edinburgh Fringe Festival and won the Scotsman's Fringe First Award and Filipa Bragança award for best solo performance.

As an Actress Emma's previous stage work includes:
New Futures (Pentabus Theatre Company), *After Orlando* (The Finborough), *Rise Up* (Belgrade, Hull Truck, Pegasus), *Upper Cut* (Southwark Playhouse), *Fast Track* (The North Wall Arts Centre), *Clean* (The Traverse Theatre and 59e59 Theaters, New York), *Crash* (North Wall Arts Centre and Arcola Theatre), *Hurried Steps* (Brighton Dome, The Cockpit Theatre, Dukes Theatre Lancaster), *A New World Order* (Shoreditch Town Hall, Barbican and Hydrocracker Theatre), *Bussin' It* (Ovalhouse Theatre, Camp Bestival) and *Millennium* (Vineyard Theatre, New York).

Previous Television and Film includes:
Trap for Cinderella (Forthcoming Productions), *BBC Ident Over the Rainbow* (Red Bee Media) and *The Naked Poet* (Triple Threat Media).

AUTHOR'S NOTE

Funeral Flowers began life as 10-minute play commissioned by the Royal Court Theatre as part of the Tottenham Festival in the summer of 2016. My brief was to write a short play working with a member of the local community and I was fortunate enough to work with Gina Moffatt, a business woman who runs the café at The Bernie Grant Arts Centre, as well as her floristry business Blooming Scent. Meeting Gina was incredible; she is full of light, love and is an exceptionally intelligent businesswoman. Gina spoke candidly about her time at HMP Holloway where she served a six year sentence. It was during her sentence that she was able to get a Prince's Trust grant to start her own business and the rest is Pride of Britain History.

Angelique's story grew from this conversation. Gina left two daughters when she went to prison, that were cared for by her family, but some young women (like Angelique) are not as fortunate and end up in the social care system.

I wanted the story to be truthful and not shy away from the realities of growing up within the care system, but I wanted people to see Angelique in all her dimensions: intelligent, ambitious and funny and like so many young women all over world she is just trying to make her own way through life. I would implore anyone taking on this play to always keep Angelique's unique light present as you tell this story.

Funeral Flowers has always been performed in a site-specific way and should bring the audience into an immersive experience. Angelique talks directly to her audience, they guide her, and this should be part of the playing of this character. The play is based in Tottenham, North London and the characters in Angelique's world are reflective of the diversity of people that inhabit the area.

Power Play is a think-tank and theatre company that uses guerrilla-style immersive theatre and data activism to examine and expose gender inequality in UK theatre.

We combine new writing programmes with data research, using narrative and numbers (the qualitative and the quantitative) to challenge the performing arts industry to diversify the stories it tells!

In 2018, *Funeral Flowers* by Emma Dennis-Edwards was part of our promenade, immersive showcase of radical plays by women, staged in a real flat in the heart of Edinburgh. Audiences were taken on a journey – in all senses – through a flat transformed by four teams of female writers and directors; reimagined in each case as the domestic backdrop to a woman's life.

This was not only a performance space, but acted as a hub for the first statistical study of gender at the Edinburgh Fringe: in fact, we think, the first research globally into gender at Fringe level theatre. The data is currently being processed, and in 2019 we are extending this research further, to update studies that look at gender inequality within the UK's most funded theatres. These studies begin to piece together insights into how women's theatre careers progress, and the systemic barriers they face.

Board of Directors:
Sophia Compton, Polly Creed and Roberto Valdo Cortese
Contact us by email: contact@powerplaytheatre.com
Or on social media: @pplaytheatre
Website: www.powerplaytheatre.com
Power Play Theatre is a Community Interest Company
(registration number 11361707).

Harts Theatre Company founded by Artistic Director, Ann Akin, in 2013 aims to produce entertaining and inspiring artistic work with outstanding artists in London.

From its inception we have also produced high quality opportunities with young and emerging talent that pushes the boundaries to shine a spotlight on unearthed talent in different areas of London.
We produce two annual festival; Young Harts Writing Festival in collaboration with Bush Theatre, which has a strong vision to break down boundaries by merging the worlds of young creatives with the professional industry and Sound Of Mind, an audio and visual arts mental wellbeing festival. We are committed to developing the arts community: developing young performers and artists in their chosen fields through professional training and support.

Artistic Director: Ann Akin
Associate Director: Roy Alexander Weise
Patron: Michael Attenborough
Advisory board: Margo Annett, Janice Beckles, Holly Smith

www.hartstheatrecompany.co.uk
@harts_theatre

Funeral Flowers was first performed at Power Play HQ, The Pleasance at the Edinburgh Fringe Festival 2018.
Funeral Flowers transferred to The Bunker Theatre, London on 15 April 2019 with the same cast and creatives.

Funeral Flowers is written to be performed by a solo performer, with the performer taking on the parts of all the characters in the text.

ANGELIQUE	Actor
WILL'S WIFE	Actor
MUM	Actor
CAROL	Actor
MICKEY	Actor
SAM	Actor
RAMPAGE	Actor

Written and Performed by Emma Dennis-Edwards
Director Rachel Nwokoro
Associate Director Sophia Compton
Producer Harts Theatre Company and Power Play

ACKNOWLEDGEMENTS

There are so many amazing people to thank for helping to bring *Funeral Flowers* alive, it really has been an incredible journey. I will start with Gina Moffatt for inspiring Angelique's story, thank you for sharing your experiences with me, and for everything you do. Our meeting wouldn't have been possible without the hard work of Chris Sonnex and Hamish Pirie, thank you for giving me the opportunity to create my own narrative and for your love and care of Angelique and the world of *Funeral Flowers*. A huge big up to the incredible Faith Alabi who first breathed life into Angelique, you're a star babygal! Thank you to my agent Kat Buckle at Curtis Brown for all of your support as an agent and friend, I really appreciate you being on this ride with me.

To the incredible Power Play Theatre Activists who took a chance on me and *Funeral Flowers*, especially Sophia Compton and the Compton clan for allowing me to complete Angelique's story in your home and garden. Rachel Nwokoro, it was a dream working with you, what a blessing of a rehearsal period, I am indebted to you.

Thank you to *The Scotsman* for seeing the potential in my show and awarding it a Fringe First Award and also to the family and friends of the late Filipa Bragança, I am so honoured to be the second actress to be awarded the Filipa Bragança Award for best solo performance. May her memory live on. And I want to especially thank Henry Naylor and Maria Luisa Bragança.

I want to thank my family and friends for always supporting my work, especially Janet, Dad, Donna, Maya, The Gilletts, Kaila, The Little Bears, East London's Finest, Shereen, Ann, Somalia, Tom, Rachael and my late grandfather Richard Edwards.

To my cousins Finley and Jaigo Edwards I think about you all the time, I love and miss you both, and I hope in the future you will come and see your big cousin's little show.

The audiences that have come to see *Funeral Flowers* who have laughed and cried with Angelique, I love each and every one of you, thank you so much for being part of this story with me and Angelique and lending your ears and eyes.

And Black Women, we always thank Black Women.

For Janet and Dad, the best parents in the world.
In loving memory of Richard Edwards.

CHARACTERS

ANGELIQUE

WILL'S WIFE

MUM

CAROL

MICKEY

SAM

RAMPAGE

ACT ONE

Tulips

ANGELIQUE My Mum is mad about Tulips.

Da way dey look, smell, feel.

Da tall stems and da elegant buds.

She lives for it.

Me? I don't mind them, they're versatile and come in loads of colours and dat.

In fact, did you know dat dey originated in Persia, which is modern day Iran?

Most people look at Tulips and fink about Amsterdam.

But der wrong,

My knowledge about Flowers is bare strong.

Cos dat's what I'm doing at college.

I can talk about flowers forever.

However, I share a name with dese... Angelique.

Not on purpose doe.

Da sperm donor AKA my Dad wanted me to call me Willow.

Da sperm donor's name is Will.

Dat's why he said Willow to name me after him.

Which is stupid cos he's never around.

Basically, when Mum went away for da first time.

I stayed with him and his wife

Truss' me I tried to be nice.

But she didn't like me much.

Kept saying I was "aggressive".

I weren't...she just like, asked me too many questions.

WILL'S WIFE Does your mum let you dress like that?

When was the last time you spoke to her?

Have you asked your Dad if that's ok?

ANGELIQUE In the end I left, ran away.

No one wants to stay where dey don't feel wanted.

Mum was only inside for five weeks that time, so it was alright in da end.

Stayed with dis Jamaican lady down in Southend.

Aunty Ava her name was and she was proper nice,

Fed me chicken and rice, pretty much everyday.

But back to my name...

I'm called Angelique because Mum wanted something that sounded a little bit more... French.

She's what is known as a Francophile.

MUM We'll go one day.

Just the two of us.

I've got it all mapped out in my head darling.

Da Eiffel Tower,

Gard du Nord,

Laudree.

We'll visit 'em all.

ANGELIQUE Dat's da thing about Mum, her head's in da clouds.

She won't be allowed to go nowhere.

Not till her probation is up and dis time that's not gonna be for a while.

So it's just nonsense for now.

A bit like how, when I told Mum what Red Tulips symbolized – true love – she was like proper haps.

MUM Yeh darling that's why I called you Angelique.

ANGELIQUE Which is lie.

Cos she only knew cos I told her.

She lies all da time,

Like I told you with France and dat.

But she's still my Mum and der's always someone worse off I guess.

Like, der's one boy at college his name is Osama Al Suq.

Didn't get much luck when it came to names.

But he's just came from Iraq dis term,

So everyone's gotta be nice to him, true he's seen a lot.

And he ain't got a Mum or a Dad.

He's deaf in one ear because of an IED.

Which I fink is proper sad.

Cos even doe da sperm donor is wotless and Mum's inside at least der not dead, you get me?

But basically, on my last visit, I upset my Mum.

I messed up and said some fings I shouldn't have said.

I said it'd be easier if she was...

You know what I'm not gonna repeat what I said, cos I didn't mean it.

See Mum ain't da strongest and I hadn't seen her in da longest,

So it was dumb of me to act like dat.

See at the moment, I'm living with Sam, she's my carer and she's cool, but it's not da same as having your Mum around.

Being "looked after" and being looked after are two different fings.

I just feel like... I dunno.

It's just kind hurts here in my chest y'know.

But that's why I love flowers doe,

Cos dey pretty much make everything better I reckon.

A lot of da girls on my floristry course ain't serious.

Der mainly here cos dey got kicked out of school.

Behavioural reports and all sorts of mad stuff like dat.

But not me, I'm here cos I want to be.

My teacher Carol, yeah, she is proper sick.

Even if she is well posh and has a funny voice.

Carol has worked for big floristry companies that have done fashion week and stuff like dat.

And guess what yeh, like a month ago she let me help her with da flowers for some girl who marrying some guy and dey were both in Love Island.

I was mainly just assisting with the decoration of da church.

But I also did da bouquet.

Da wedding was featured in OK,

Which is a trashy mag but it's still coverage so it's kinda cool.

I'd never been to a wedding before.

Carol was like.

CAROL   It's so vulgar darling, these flower walls make me feel positively sick... White roses are such a cliché. And as for the mother of the bride... Mutton dressed up as lamb. Wait til you start doing fashion week, that's where it's at!

ANGELIQUE   I nodded my head like Yeah.

But really I thought da church looked beautiful. So did da bride.

Carol is obviously over it.

She's been married like three times.

Which is kinda a good fing because dat means three dudes wanted to marry her.

I don't reckon I'd be able to convince da one.

Well not da one I've got anyways.

Since Mum went away again and I've been living with Sam, he don't check for me.

I see him in college but he claims he's a "private person" don't want everyone in our business.

Which I get, yet I still feel a way.

Cos even doe it's been half a year, half our year don't know.

I reckon I probably love him, dat's why I put up with his shit.

Cos he's ain't a hit with Mum.

MUM You can do better darling. Get a boy with some prospects.

ANGELIQUE Which I fink is a bit unfair.

Yeh, he might not have done good at school.

But he makes funny jokes, and he's good at art.

He's going to start a YouTube channel soon, and people who do dat make bare money.

Especially if der as piff as him.

Da fing is he rolls with a bad crowd.

It's fine when I'm around.

But lately he's been rolling with dem deep.

See Mickey – dat's my boyfriend – owes Rampage a favour.

Rampage is boss man and sells drugs to all of da ravers.

White kids who keep moving into da luxury flats, kids from places like Berkshire who like to do da dab.

And also like a dab of coke, or smoke a bit of weed or take some E's.

See, Rampage is bad news.

Mickey's kinda shook, as he's only a younger in da crew.

Rampage is like God to him.

So what it is, Rampage liked my pics on instagram.

Underneath one of dem he wrote some comment saying he would bang.

And I was like nahhhhh. Dead dat still.

One, I've got a man, and two, Rampage is like proper old.

Like at least twenty-four.

Rampage told Mickey dat he's been taking liberties,

And that Mickey owes him bare peas,

Cos Mickey was meant to take a couple of keys down country but he never.

See Mickey can't leave his Nan for too long.

Cos she's not all der and she's also a bit racist.

Now dis is where it gets proper mad.

Mickey was like.

MICKEY Babes, you can help me clear a couple debts.

ANGELIQUE I mean I probably wouldn't have to do like full...

Just let Rampage feel me up a bit.

At first I was like.

What kinda Fuckery?

Are you mad in your head?

Do I look any yat?

I've got dreams and ambitions and dat.

I'm gonna be like a businesswoman one day.

See me with Richard Branson, Karen Brady, Patricia Bright and probably who ever is Prime Minister at da time.

Don't try and mug me off you prick.

MICKEY If you don't den I understand, but Angelique you'll be making my funeral flowers.

ANGELIQUE Men are a fucking joke.

I mean look at dis madness Mickey has got me into.

I don't really know what to do.

And I don't really have no one cos Mum's away.

Mickey ain't perfect but at least he stays.

Cos that day when Mum was in court, I skipped college to go,

And it was some next ends in south and they wouldn't let me in.

But Mickey came through.

Held my hand da whole time outside da court and told me it was going to be alright.

Even doe da day before we'd have a fight, about suttin' stupid I can't even remember.

And Mickey ain't got no one apart from me.

Well he's got his Nan.

But like I said she's mad and a bit racist, so it's all a bit long.

So probably if I'm honest it's like we belong.

Mum did say dat family comes first but she doesn't always practice what she preaches.

Cos is she did, she'd be here not der.

Cos when her and her boyfriend were making money dey didn't care.

Weren't finking about what might happen if he got caught.

Defo weren't finking about me.

Now it's gonna be time till she comes back.

I've got a savings goal.

Twenty thousand pounds in four years.

That's enough paper to proper set up my own floristry business.

If the bank like match it of course. Which they will.

With the income from dat, I'd be able to get me and mum a flat.

Once Mum comes home it's gonna be the two of us again.

No more men...

I wanna talk to mum about everything but she won't understand.

And it's not the kinda fing you can talk to your mum about.

So I guess I'm gonna have to figure it out by myself.

ACT TWO

Lilies

ANGELIQUE I dunno why, but I really hate it when people make judgements when dey don't know shit.

Do you know what I mean?

It's like, if you say you like Lilies people fink you're some kind of morbid weirdo.

Cos of the way how Lilies are associated with funerals and death and dat.

But actually if you deep it real quick, Lilies are actually about innocence.

Lilies represent the soul departing the body and giving new innocence to da person who has died.

It's kinda dat way with Sam, the woman who I live with.

People make judgements about her cos

She's a "queer".

No it's alright – I checked with her it's alright to say dat.

Cos that's what it – sorry *she* is.

Sorry nah, part of who she is.

It's one of the excuses dat Mickey makes to not come around.

MICKEY Not being funny yeah but I can't be around dose kind of people der.

ANGELIQUE Dat's one of da fings I don't like about Mickey.

He's so narrow-minded.

I really like Sam.

She's been teaching me lots of stuff about feminism and Green politics.

She can't cook for shit.

And her clothes are dead, but she's kind.

Dis is her first time fostering.

And she got me.

When I first arrived she had one rule.

SAM   You'll be 18 soon, so I'm not gonna patronise you, but I want you to respect me and this house and everything inside it. So that means we're honest with each other, we don't lie. I'm transparent with you and you do the same to me.

ANGELIQUE   And I think mostly I have.

Apart from da couple of times I sneaked out to see Mickey.

And the night he stayed over and we got caught.

But, nah, see that wasn't my fault.

His Nan who is mental had locked him out.

And I didn't want him out and about, getting into trouble.

Sam was clear that he couldn't stay. Mickey was like:

MICKEY   It's cos she's gay.

ANGELIQUE   But it's not, it's got nothing to do with dat,

Dat's just her rules which I fink are fair enough.

Even doe she was proper tough on me da next day.

Said I'd broken her trust and dat I'd hurt her by lying.

I felt so bad but I didn't say anything.

The fing is... I'd do it again.

So I don't want to say sorry cos dat feels like lying.

Dat's da fing with Mickey, I don't seem to be able to say No to him ever.

Like da first time we...you know.

I didn't really want to.

Not because it was him, cos he's bare sexy.

But da circumstances were kinda weird; he'd sneaked me into his Nan's house.

She was in bed because it was quite late at night.

Der's a picture of him when he's little in da hallway,

With a black eye – he probably got in a fight.

It made me fink der aren't many pictures of me as a kid.

We've moved around so much and Mum couldn't always afford to put stuff in storage so fings had to go.

But I proper love looking at people's baby photos.

He took me to his room and lies me down on the bed.

MICKEY   Don't make too much noise yeh. Cos she's a light sleeper.

ANGELIQUE   It was quick, but it's better now.

Now that we know each other better.

So it's ok. Better then OK, it's great.

He wants me to come over tonight.

His Nan's gone to Billericay to visit his Aunt.

Bare people from college are gonna be der.

After half a year, dis is da moment I've been waiting for.

Sam said I can't because, college,

But I can't just not go.

So I'm gonna have to sneak out.

Mickey told me to be der at around nine.

But I can't, because I've got to make sure Sam is asleep before I go.

He rings me so many times, y'know.

I hate it when he does dis.

He's gonna get nasty soon.

If he doesn't get his own way he starts saying stuff to me.

Like horrible stuff.

I hate it.

He makes me feel like shit

Questions my loyalty.

Some of the shit he accuses me of is proper fucked.

MICKEY Everyone says to me I shouldn't even be with you cos of your reputation.

You've fucked so many guys Angelique, and yet I'm still here with you.

ANGELIQUE Half da shit he says ain't even true.

I've not had sex with half as many people as he has.

Apparently it's different because I'm a girl.

So I have to go, don't I?

It's 1 am when I get der and da party's in full swing.

I go inside and look for him.

As I walk through the crowd I feel a hand on my waist.

I smile and turn around.

MICKEY It's Rampage.

RAMPAGE What you saying?

ANGELIQUE Not a lot.

You seen Mickey?

RAMPAGE Last time I saw him he was in his room...with Lauren.

ANGELIQUE At this stage I practically run to his room.

I hate Lauren.

Mickey knows I do.

She used to be ok when we were in Primary school,

But in Secondary she made my life hell,

Always chatting shit about me to da other girls.

Saying that Mum's a crackhead.

Mum might be in prison, but she's a hundred percent not on crack.

So it is fucked to say stuff like dat.

She also started dis rumour that I was slag in Year Nine.

Which is crazy cos I didn't even lose my V plates till Year Ten.

Everyone believed her doe.

Mickey knows.

If he's up der with her I'll go mad.

I burst into da room don't even knock.

Mickey's lying down on his bed looking up.

MICKEY Babe, I'm fucked.

ANGELIQUE I dunno why he does this he can't handle his drink.

I sink into the bed.

I lie down next to him and hold his hand.

Together we block out all the noise and it's just us.

I forget about Lauren, Rampage, Mum and Sam.

Cos dis right here.

Is da only fing dat matters,

Dis feeling that I have right here.

I know he feels it too.

MICKEY Rampage is here and he's bought his whole crew.

ANGELIQUE I just saw him doe, I think you're alright.

He's not gonna do something tonight is he? Not with everyone around.

MICKEY I'm scared babe. The only reason why he ain't done me in yet is cos of you.

ANGELIQUE I just can't.

I want to help.

But not in dat way.

We'll figure out another plan babe.

How much do you owe him?

I've got savings, I didn't want to say.

I'd help you.

You'd have to pay me back.

Mickey smiles and starts kissing me,

Hard. Kissing me hard and I can't breathe.

I try to push him off but he's not going to stop.

He can't stop.

He won't stop.

I fucking freeze.

He don't doe.

He's moving bare fast,

And I feel sick.

He lifts my top over my head, pushes me down hard onto da bed.

Suddenly he stops.

MICKEY Have a drink.

ANGELIQUE He grabs a bottle of Appleton from the side of da bed.

I'm alright babe, I've got college in the morning.

MICKEY Open. Your. Mouth.

ANGELIQUE He pours it down my throat.

It burns.

Stop! I can't drink anymore.

He won't stop.

He can't stop.

We're kissing again and my head hurts and my eyes are stinging.

And it's like da first time again.

But without da funny butterflies or his Nan being next door.

And dis time it feels long, not quick like da first time.

Everything hurts.

And I don't know if it's da drink,

But I'm starting to fink like something is wrong.

I put my clothes back on and the silence is scaring me so I try to break it.

Are you alright, Babe?

He doesn't answer me.

Picks up da bottle and drinks it.

Then walks to the door, which is a little bit open and

Rampage is standing there filming on his phone.

He pats Mickey on da back and says:

RAMPAGE Nice show.

ANGELIQUE Der's a video?

Mickey did you know?

Answer me.

Mickey shrugs his shoulders and walks off.

Rampage is laughing his head off.

Mickey!

I try to push past Rampage but he blocks my path.

RAMPAGE Not so fast. Now that I've seen you in action, I think I want a go.

ANGELIQUE No!

But da words don't come out.

In my head I'm shouting really loud.

All my muscles seem to be dead.

I'm back lying on da bed.

Dis time face down.

I can't even feel anything anymore.

I just want everything to stop.

And I want to be at college with my flowers.

Or in my bed.

Or talking to Sam.

Just anywhere but here.

I want to be anyone but me right now.

I hate myself.

I really fucking do.

I feel a spurt of warm liquid on the back of my thigh.

RAMPAGE Pull out game strong.

ANGELIQUE Den he's gone.

I don't know how but I've got to leave too.

I walk past that picture of Mickey in the hallway with his black eye.

Open the door and I go outside.

The cold air hits me.

Mickey's outside with Lauren.

Got his arm around her and she's laughing.

It's weird because in this moment in time, I don't even care.

He catches my eye and takes his arm from around her.

MICKEY Angelique.

ANGELIQUE But I keep on walking.

I walk da 2 miles to Sam's house and it's nearly daylight now.

I look at my phone der's 17 missed calls.

Sam. My social worker.

Before I put my keys in, Sam opens da door.

SAM Where have you been?

ANGELIQUE I can't tell her da truth.

I can't tell her what happened.

She'll probably say it's my fault for sneaking out.

So it's better dat I don't say anything.

I can't cope with her right now.

I can practically see da disgust in her eyes.

She's knows that I'm dirty and soiled inside.

SAM Angelique, I'm talking to you. I was so worried I was going to call the police.

Are you drunk?

ANGELIQUE Yeah.

SAM You promised me Angelique; this is why I said no in the first place. Did you go round Mickeys?

ANGELIQUE It's none of your business, leave me alone!

SAM Did you even check your phone, I left you so many missed calls. Angelique we can't go on like this. Look at the state of you.

ANGELIQUE I don't know what it is but I start to get real mad.

So I say to Sam.

You're not my Mum or my Dad.

You're just a dyke with no life, no kids of your own.

Scoring a quick cheque, by opening your home,

To little fuckers like me.

Well no one said it was gonna be easy.

SAM Do not call me names Angelique.

ANGELIQUE I'll say what I want.

I'll do what I want.

I don't need you or anyone telling me what to do.

I'm going to have a shower now, I've got college at 9.

Is that allowed or do you want to watch me take a shower?

Cos you seem to want to watch my every move.

You fancy me or something?

SAM Don't be disgusting.

ANGELIQUE I'm disgusting.

I'm fucking disgusting.

You're a fucking sham.

Look at you half woman and half man.

Leave me the fuck alone.

I go to the bathroom run myself a shower.

Turn the hot water on and turn da knob to da fullest power.

As the water burns my skin, I'm still not clean.

I can smell Mickey mixed with Rampage.

And all over my skin I see bits of dirt,

Like soil.

And then I know I'm really waved because little lillies are sprouting through my skin.

I vomit den.

Den dey disappear.

But I'm not innocent again.

ACT THREE

Fair Trade White Roses

ANGELIQUE It's been over a week and we ain't spoken at all.

Mickey is ignoring my calls,

And my WhatsApps.

Leaving me on read.

After day three, I panic and fink he must be dead.

Rampage finally got him.

And I was wrong to blame him for what happened.

Day four, he changes his WhatsApp profile picture so I know he's alive.

He just doesn't want to talk to me.

It's worse now da video's out.

I've not been to college since dat night.

I just can't face it.

Everyone's seen me.

Dey don't care that Mickey's my boyfriend – was my boyfriend.

It just proves what dey all already knew.

Dat I'm dirty.

Dat I got fucked by two guys in one night.

Even doe I didn't want to.

Mostly I just stay in my room.

Sam is barely talking to me, after I called her every name under da sun.

I fink it might be time for me to move on.

Der's an assisted living place a little bit further north, a space has opened up, I can move in a couple days' time.

Maybe I can start again.

Spoke to my social worker and

There's a local college where I can continue my course.

But I'll need a reference. I ask to meet Carol.

I can't face college so I meet her in a café in her area.

Muswell Hill. Well fancy.

CAROL Darling we've not seen you in ages. Where the fuck have you been?

ANGELIQUE I've been busy.

CAROL Doing what? Come on don't give me that shit.

ANGELIQUE I need a reference. I'm moving in a couple weeks and can't be coming back round here...it's long.

CAROL Ok, I'll see what I can do... I'm going to miss you Angelique, you've been one of my favourite students. Much prefer you to half those idiots in that class. You have a real talent darling, don't waste it.

ANGELIQUE I swear to you, I won't, I've just got to get out.

Den I don't know why, but I start to cry.

And I know that she knows.

About the video.

CAROL You know you can talk to me.

ANGELIQUE I can't.

Carol nods her head.

Promises to ring da college for me da next day, the head of the course is an old colleague.

CAROL He's a twat but he knows his stuff. See you around kiddo. Anything you need let me know.

ANGELIQUE And just like dat she's gone.

Everything is temporary like flowers I guess.

The growth comes before da death.

I'm defo a little bit dead inside.

But I literally can't hide forever.

I want to tell Sam so bad,

I think she knows something is up.

If I told her maybe she'll understand dat night when I said all dose horrible fings that I didn't even mean.

To be honest I think she's glad to see the back of me and I don't blame her.

Will you drop me der... Please?

SAM If you want.

ANGELIQUE Thanks.

She doesn't have to. I'm entitled to a cab to move my stuff.

But I figured if she drives me I can apologise properly.

I wanted to make Sam a nice bouquet of white roses but I've not been in college so I don't have any to make it.

She told me once dey were her favourites.

When I first moved in.

It's one of the first fings I ask people.

New beginnings.

SAM You what?

ANGELIQUE White roses that's new beginnings, dat's what dey represent.

SAM I didn't know that, I guess it's a new start for you and me.

ANGELIQUE I wonder if that moment she knew how fings would end up.

Just how fucked up, it would all get.

I fink I always did.

Me and Sam sit in da car.

I fink der's something dat you need to know.

It's not easy to say dis but dat night when I...

When I said all dat stuff... I'm...

Der's no excuses.

You're an amazing person and you deserve better. And...

Thank you for everything you've done.

Sam don't say nothing but she has tears in her eyes.

And I'm worried cos she driving and don't want her to crash, so I just kinda wipe.

But at da same time it's not all doom and gloom.

Mum's coming out soon.

She's been a model prisoner.

And half her sentence is up.

I'm gonna get her.

I've not seen her for ages.

I told her dat I'd moved but didn't tell her about all da Mickey stuff.

Or the video.

Or the stuff with Sam.

I was gonna...

But when I opened my mouth da words wouldn't come out.

It's like dat night happening all over again and I can't block it out.

But I have to.

ACT FOUR

Sunflowers

ANGELIQUE When I sort out my first place, like proper place not hostel.

A place with like a long corridor.

With one of dem side tables, and on dat side table is a big blue vase.

The first fing you'll see are Sunflowers.

Sunflowers are mad underrated, people fink der basic.

A bit common.

But dey look amazing.

I want dat brightness for Mum.

Especially coming from where she's coming from.

It took me a while to settle into fings in here but I keep myself to myself.

All da women who work here don't seem much older than us.

But dat don't mean der soft, der's loads of rules.

Der's a timetable for washing clothes,

A rota for cleaning,

A curfew,

You can't have boys or friends or anyone round.

Which suits me fine.

I don't have a boy or friends or anyone.

Just got myself and my flowers and I'm alright like dat.

Mostly people just let you down.

I can't stay with Mum when she comes out, not till I'm 18 cos she not my legal guardian anymore.

I think it's best, get herself back on her feet.

Less pressure on her.

It took 2 trains and a coach to reach, and I'd brought Mum a massive bouquet.

Sunflowers of course.

I sign in and wait.

It's fucked because dey searched da bouquet.

Feds.

Der something else honestly.

As well as the bouquet I brought her a little suitcase, so she don't feel embarrassed when she comes out.

Because dey just give you a see through bag so it's kinda embarrassing.

Everyone knows where you've been.

So when Mum comes out finally it was kinda awkward because I don't have no spare hands so we just kinda air kiss.

Mum what you crying for?

MUM I can't help it babe, you look so much older.

I've missed you so much, and I'll never make it up.

ANGELIQUE I dunno what to say cos it's true.

I'm a different girl to da one she left.

Where you staying?

MUM Edmonton for 2 weeks, then somewhere a bit more permanent hopefully.

See what probation say.

ANGELIQUE OK.

MUM Only temporary lovely, then I'll find us somewhere.

ANGELIQUE I've got somewhere.

MUM You need to be with your mum.

ANGELIQUE Which is a dumb thing to say. Because we both know it's da other way.

But I don't wanna argue so I just say OK.

The journey back is super long,

Mum is going on about her prison job *(cleaning)*

Some bitch who kept nicking her make up *(Karen)*

And about France.

I don't say much,

Sounds like she's had a grand old fucking time in prison.

A whole little life she's had.

Jobs and gossip,

Friends and food,

Cookery and drama classes.

While I've been moved from pillar to post,

She's been doing da most.

Right little jail socialite.

MUM Everything alright?

ANGELIQUE Peachy.

MUM Not with that stupid boy –

ANGELIQUE We broke up. I don't wanna talk about it.

You still with yours?

She stays silent.

What a fucking joke.

I'm fuming right now.

Eventually we get to Mum's place and it looks quite crap.

It's a hostel same as mine, but da people staying der look kinda rough.

Cracks on the walls, crackheads walking along da lino floor.

I see her face and for da first time she looks unsure.

I would let you stay at mine Mum but dey don't let us have people stay overnight.

MUM It's alright.

ANGELIQUE Well I'm gonna say bye.

I give Mum a hug, put her flowers on da little shelf.

I'll come tomorrow after college.

I get another bus back to mine and I'm ready for my bed.

But sitting outside on the wall it's him.

Mickey.

You've got to be kidding.

MICKEY I've been waiting outside for time, they wouldn't let me in.

What kind of place is this?

Eh? Angelique? Say something babe.

ANGELIQUE He goes to give me a hug.

I move away cos I'm not a fucking mug.

Get you hands off me.

MICKEY Rah, I weren't gonna do nothing.

ANGELIQUE What do you want?

MICKEY I dunno, to see you I guess.

ANGELIQUE How'd you find me?

MICKEY I've got this cousin, Tess.

She goes your college she's doing hairdressing or something. Asked if she seen a black girl doing floristry and I guess you're the only one.

ANGELIQUE How come?

What you asking about me for?

MICKEY Aite Boom...we didn't end of good terms, I hate dat
fings got so fucked up.

You see that night? I was proper drunk... I never thought
you'd actually go through with it.

But now that you have it's all kind of mad.

ANGELIQUE I did it for you.

You said you wouldn't let it go too far.

You told me you loved me and dat it would be alright.

But dat night...

I'll never be the same.

I feel like I'm...stained.

Den it gets weird and he starts to cry.

He's crying so much I feel kinda bad.

So I hold him,

Bearing in mind we're on the street and dat.

MICKEY I'm sorry.

I really did care,

I wish I could have been der for you.

But da video made things complicated.

ANGELIQUE Well I hope you're happy now.

Cleared off you debts.

MICKEY Not quite, dat's da ting I wanted to ask you.

On dat night,

You said you might be able to help man.

Dat you had some savings,

I just need a couple peas.

Please Angelique, I ain't got no one else to ask.

ANGELIQUE I start to see Mickey for the first time.

He's still dat little boy with a black eye.

Even I ain't much, I'm better than him.

And maybe I always have been.

Fuck you Mickey.

I hope Rampage slits your throat.

His phone rings, I see the name flash up:

Lauren.

I turn and walk away.

MICKEY Angelique! ANGELIQUE!

ANGELIQUE I go inside and shut da door to my room.

And da perfume of my flowers make me feel safe again.

I wait for da tears to come but I just feel numb,

And cold,

I'm 17 years old,

Just trying to nurture my seeds.

And maybe I'm more a weed den a flower.

But I'm still here.

I'll rise through da dirt,

Even when it hurts.

And it hurts.

But I'm still here.

But when I close my eyes.

I can see da prize.

I can see a pair of Red bottoms on my feet.

And I'm doing all the final details cos it's fashion week.

Or I like see:

"Angelique's flowers" over a huge duck-egg blue sign.

And florists wearing aprons dat say da same thing as mine.

And people happy when dey come in my shop.

Cos it's full of flowers.

Funeral Flowers,

Wedding Flowers,

Birthday Flowers,

And I'm da boss.

I dream big.

Maybe I'm more like my Mum den I think.

End

VISIT THE
SAMUEL FRENCH
BOOKSHOP
AT THE
ROYAL COURT THEATRE

Browse plays and theatre books, get expert advice and enjoy a coffee

Samuel French Bookshop
Royal Court Theatre
Sloane Square
London
SW1W 8AS
020 7565 5024

Shop from thousands of titles on our website

 samuelfrench.co.uk

 samuelfrenchltd

 samuel french uk

Lightning Source UK Ltd.
Milton Keynes UK
UKHW020738190519
342860UK00006B/318/P

9 780573 116209